the
joy of
now
JOURNAL

www.stmartins.com
www.castlepointbooks.com

The Castle Point Books trademark is owned by
Castle Point Publications, LLC.
Castle Point books are published and distributed by St. Martin's Press.

ISBN 978-1-250-16344-8 (trade paperback)

Design by Katie Jennings Campbell

Images used under license from Shutterstock.com

Our books may be purchased in bulk for promotional, educational, or business use.
Please contact your local bookseller or the Macmillan Corporate and
Premium Sales Department at 1-800-221-7945, extension 5442,
or by e-mail at MacmillanSpecialMarkets@macmillan.com.

First Edition: January 2018

10 9 8 7 6 5 4 3 2 1

the joy of now

JOURNAL

mindfulness
in five
minutes
a day

PAIGE BURKES

Castle Point Books
New York

live beyond
"what if."
find joy in
"what is."

introduction

DO MORE. BE MORE. ACCUMULATE MORE. That's the mistaken path we often try to take toward happiness. But pure joy is right here, right now, waiting for you through the practice of mindfulness.

What is mindfulness? It's simply slowing down enough to notice, without judgment, all the little things inside and around you that are occurring in the present moment. And it can be practiced by anyone, at any time, to help you live life to the fullest.

The Joy of Now is your guide along your journey into mindfulness. With inspiration and simple exercises on every page, you'll awaken to opportunities for joy in every moment of your day—body, mind, spirit, relationships, finances, and career. All it takes is five minutes each day for change that can last a lifetime.

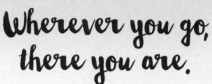

*Wherever you go,
there you are.*

—Jon Kabat-Zinn

Many people travel or move to new locales to change
their lives, thinking that new surroundings will create
a completely different life. You are still the same person wherever you go. The outside environment may
change, but until your internal environment changes,
you'll make the same choices, attract the same kinds
of people, and have the same kinds of experiences.

What places do you need to mark as off-limits?
Put an **X** through them.

Anger   Self-Doubt   Resentment

          Negativity   Guilt   Fear
Regret
          Comparison   Worry

Busyness   Seeking Worth
                  from the World

What places do you need to spend more time exploring?
Circle them.

Adventure   Passion

                    Soul
Knowledge   Restoration   Spontaneity

Intuition   Connections   Balance

          Self-Care   Creativity

               Discovery

Our lives are lived
in intense and
anxious struggle,
in a swirl of speed
and aggression,
in competing,
grasping, possessing
and achieving,
forever burdening
ourselves with
extraneous activities
and preoccupations.

—Sogyal Rinpoche

What are five things, tasks, worries, or people
you could live without for the next week?

Release them here
and in your life,
then notice
what happens.

2. _____

3. _____

1. _____

4. _____

5. _____

Life begins at the end of

your
comfort
zone.

-Neale Donald Walsch

What small step can you take
outside of your comfort zone today?

And what bigger step
will you take tomorrow?

What are the first five things you notice when you
enter your home after being gone all day?
Consider sights, smells, sounds, feelings.

1. _____
2. _____
3. _____
4. _____
5. _____

What would you *like* to experience
when you arrive home?

_____
_____
_____
_____
_____

What small changes can you make to create the
"coming home" experience you envision?

_____
_____
_____
_____

Happiness
is homemade.

Sometimes we create
our own heartbreaks
through expectations.

Expectations can rob us of joy. When people and circumstances don't obey our rules, we can feel the full range of negative emotions, from anger and disappointment to envy and bitterness. Without expectations, acceptance of what is would be infinitely easier.

In the past week, how have your
expectations robbed you of joy?

Draw a picture of what was in your head
versus what the reality turned out to be.

How can you change or release your expectations today?

Possibilities in life
are endless; we are all
surrounded by them.
But a negative mind
fails to see them,
because it is incapable
of looking beyond
its present obstacles.

—Edmond Mbiaka

List five recent disappointments or obstacles you've faced. What have you learned from each of them? What can you now accept, feel grateful for, and appreciate about each of them?

1. _____
Learning that leads to joy: _____

2. _____
Learning that leads to joy: _____

3. _____
Learning that leads to joy: _____

4. _____
Learning that leads to joy: _____

5. _____
Learning that leads to joy: _____

Whenever you experience a disappointment, large or small, repeat this exercise.

If we learn to open
our hearts, anyone,
including the people
who drive us crazy,
can be our teacher.

—Pema Chödrön

Make a list of five people you'll see today.

Include a few who tend to challenge your patience.
(Can you feel compassion for them instead of annoyance?)
For each person, write how you'll let them know how much
you appreciate them and what you appreciate them for.
As you see each person, be sure to do what you wrote.

1. _____ _____

_____

_____

2. _____

_____

_____

3. _____

_____

_____

4. _____

_____

_____

5. _____

_____

_____

If you concentrate
on finding whatever is good
in every situation,
you will discover
that your life will
suddenly be filled with

gratitude

a feeling that
nurtures the soul.

—Rabbi Harold Kushner

List ten simple things you're grateful for now
and why you're grateful for each one.

1. _____
_____
2. _____
_____
3. _____
_____
4. _____
_____
5. _____
_____
6. _____
_____
7. _____
_____
8. _____
_____
9. _____
_____
10. _____
_____

Right now you
have everything
you need to be
in bliss.

—Anthony de Mello

Whose rules have you adopted that tell you that
you can't be happy with what you have now?

Is that person truly happy?

What would it feel like to be happy in this moment?
Are you willing to throw out those old rules to allow it?

Yesterday's the past,
tomorrow's the future,
but today is a gift.
That's why it's
called the present.

—Bil Keane

What small gift have you been denying yourself?

- [ ] *time just for you*
- [ ] *forgiveness*
- [ ] **acceptance of praise**
- [ ] *nurturing friendships*
- [ ] *permission to love*
- [ ] *risk-taking*
- [ ] *the ability to say no*
- [ ] _____
- [ ] _____
- [ ] _____
- [ ] _____
- [ ] _____

Give yourself that gift today.
And while you're at it, share it with someone else.

When you do things from your soul, you feel a river moving in you, a joy.

—Jalaluddin Rumi

The common societal programming dictates that fun, play, and creativity must be postponed indefinitely until all the work is done. What kind of life has that created for you?

Carve out at least ten minutes today to do something for which your soul yearns. Write about how you felt afterward.

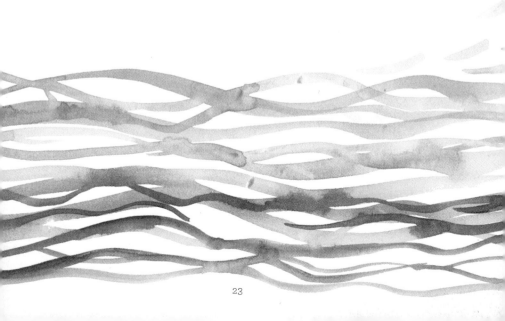

The moment one gives
close attention to anything,
even a blade of grass,
it becomes a mysterious,
awesome, indescribably
magnificent world in itself.

—Henry Miller

Choose a leaf of any kind.

Look at it closely, smell it, feel it, experience it. Without making positive or negative assessments of the leaf, simply notice its characteristics. Sketch the leaf or write the words that come to mind to describe it below. Spend at least five minutes with the leaf, aiming to keep your thoughts only of it.

When you're tempted to lose focus on the good throughout the week, remember the leaf as a way to center your thoughts.

It's not about time,

How are you
spending
your choices?

—Beverly Adamo

it's about choices.

Every little choice you make throughout your day is creating
your tomorrow and your life. Things you may think are out of
your control, like your thoughts and feelings, are completely
in your power. They are choices you're making.

Reflect on your day.

What choices have you made so far?

When did you wake up? What have you eaten?

Whom have you interacted with? What activities have you done?

What did you choose to work on first in your day?

The outcomes of these choices lead to certain results
in your emotions, thoughts, beliefs, and subsequent actions.
What results are you experiencing? Are these the results you want?

Your Way

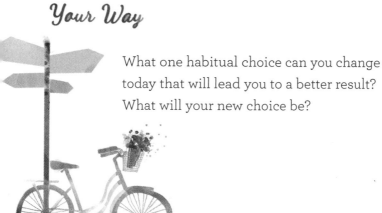

What one habitual choice can you change
today that will lead you to a better result?
What will your new choice be?

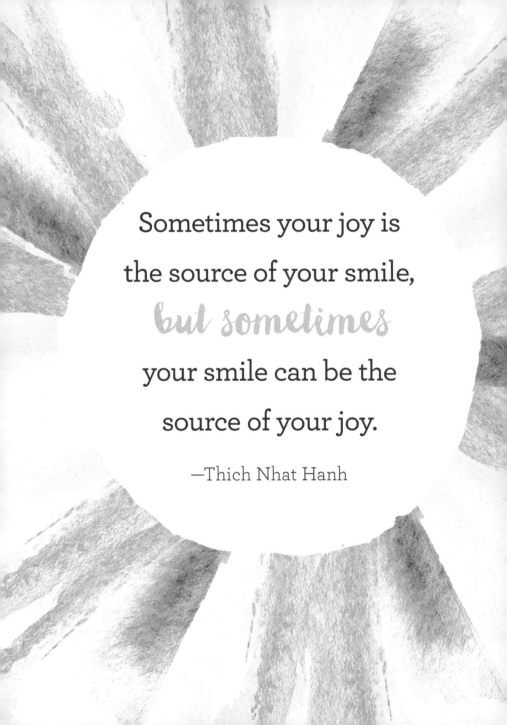

Sometimes your joy is
the source of your smile,
but sometimes
your smile can be the
source of your joy.

—Thich Nhat Hanh

Your physical state significantly influences your feelings and emotions. If you're in a bad mood, you can choose to change it to something better. Smile for thirty seconds (especially if you don't feel like it) and see how you feel. Or do something active and uplifting and see how long you can maintain that bad mood. Choosing new activities can change your emotions, which changes your thoughts, which changes your actions.

List some of your favorite activities or positive actions you can use to encourage a better mood when you need it.

Don't delay your joy.

How many times have you said or thought about a lingering project or nagging task, "When this is done, I'll be happy"?

Make a plan to accomplish whatever it is that you've been procrastinating about. If you can't complete the task today, at least form the full plan to work toward completion within the foreseeable future. Unfinished business can be handcuffs on happiness.

The dreaded deadline:

My plan to finish and remove the weight:

Any resources I still need:

Don't underestimate
the value of
Doing Nothing,
of just going along,
listening to all the
things you can't hear,
and not bothering.

—Winnie the Pooh

When was the last time you did nothing?

In the world of doing, doing, doing, it can be difficult to imagine simply being. Society says that being isn't productive; it's a "waste of time."

Mindfulness is the art of being. In mindfulness, there is no doing.

Schedule five minutes today to do nothing but notice and daydream.

to Do List

- ☐ NOTHING _____
- ☐ _____
- ☐ _____

The only difference between a flower and a weed is judgment.

—Wayne Dyer

Mindfulness is noticing without judging.

It's difficult not to judge. But when you can get past it, you find more joy. Judging can include labeling things and people as good, bad, normal, strange, or any other descriptor. Notice where your judging mind takes you throughout your day.

What I saw

_____

My initial reaction (judgment)

_____

_____

How I can think differently

_____

_____

What I saw

_____

My initial reaction (judgment)

_____

_____

How I can think differently

_____

_____

Do small things
with great love.

—Mother Teresa

Sometimes life can seem so overwhelming.

You want to pursue joy for yourself and others, but you don't know where to start. The good news: you can start anywhere. You don't need to be a superhero who saves the world.

Try simply writing a short thank-you note today to someone who isn't expecting it. Let them know the positive impact they've had on you. Plan whom you'll write by marking their name on the envelope.

Almost everything
will work again if you
unplug it for a few minutes,
including you.

—Anne Lamott

Weekends are the perfect time to slow down, unplug, recharge, and tune back in to yourself and pure joy.

Choose one full day to completely unplug from all devices. The world won't end if you don't immediately respond to every call, text, email, or tweet. Give yourself this gift, then notice and journal about how you feel because of it. Anxious? Relaxed? Relieved? Why do you feel the way you do? How can you take what you've learned into your week?

At the end of the day,
your feet should be dirty,
your hair messy, and
your eyes sparkling.

—Shanti Devi

Spending time in nature has the power to bring us back to simple beauty. Research actually shows that it can induce a relaxation response.

How can you plan to soak in more nature today?

☐ Open your windows wide

☐ Enjoy meals outside

☐ Take a walk instead of a coffee break

☐ Move your work and meetings outside when you can

☐ Spend time gardening

☐ Try birdwatching

☐ Go on a hike or photo walk

☐ Volunteer to clean up a trail or road near you

☐ Play outside with your dog (or a friend's)

☐ Paint or sketch in nature

☐ Find the perfect outdoor reading nook

☐ _____

☐ _____

☐ _____

☐ _____

The older I get,
the more I realize I just
need the simple things in life:

a comfy home,
good food on the table,
and to be surrounded
by the people I love.

—David Wolfe

Choose a day to eat at least one meal (or all of them) slowly and in silence, mindfully aware of every aspect of your food and drink. What does it...

Look like? Smell like? Taste like? Feel like?

_____

_____

_____

_____

How do you feel as you're consuming it?

_____

_____

_____

_____

How do you feel afterward?

_____

_____

_____

_____

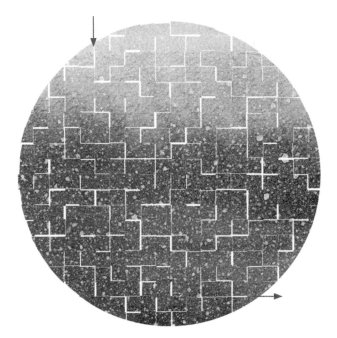

Finish each
day and be
done with it.

—Ralph Waldo Emerson

Writing out your thoughts by hand helps you to move beyond the endless thought cycles that go nowhere and keep you stuck. Journal about something that's been spinning in your head for a while. Don't stop until you've exhausted every thought you could possibly have about the issue. You'll help free your mind of the burden and open more space to experience joy.

Twenty years from now you will be
more disappointed by the things that you
didn't do than by the ones you did do.
So throw off the bowlines.
Sail away from the safe harbor.
Catch the trade winds in your sails.

Explore. Dream. Discover.

—Mark Twain

You can celebrate the joy of each day you're given with some relatively simple choices. Resolve to stop waiting for the perfect time or occasion to...

- ✓ Take a new path to a familiar place
- ✓ Try a new (exotic) food or restaurant
- ✓ Use the "good" dishes—go ahead and drink your OJ out of a champagne glass
- ✓ Wear sequins
- ✓ Light candles in the bedroom
- ✓ Learn a new language

Ready for bigger, bolder steps?

- ✓ Start writing the Great American Novel
- ✓ Book your dream vacation
- ✓ Reconnect with someone you haven't spoken with in years
- ✓ Have your portrait drawn or taken

How will you celebrate life in the next few days?

_____

_____

_____

_____

The little things?
The little moments?

They aren't little.

—Jon Kabat-Zinn

Our lives are composed of an endless number of moments, most of them little. A glance. A few words. A breathtaking scene. A touch. Each of these may seem little, but what would life be without them?

Make a list of eight "little" things or moments that have been memorable or have positively impacted your life.

As you go through your day, notice how many of these types of little moments you encounter that you may not have noticed before.

Do what you can,
where you are,
with what you have.

—Theodore Roosevelt

Meditation can help you to slow down and notice the present moment in all its beautiful detail.

Sit in a comfortable position with your back straight, hands resting comfortably in your lap. Close your eyes. Take three deep breaths as you relax. Relax your face, your jaw, your shoulders, and your back. Continue to breathe deeply a few more times, noticing how your breath feels moving in and out of your nostrils and your lungs. Sit and breathe normally for five minutes.

Notice the thoughts that move through your mind. Notice the emotions you experience. Try not to judge your thoughts, your emotions, or yourself. Watch them all come and go like clouds drifting across the blue sky. Notice how the thoughts and emotions are not you. They are all things that pass by in time when you choose to allow them.

If people sat outside and looked at the stars each night, I'll bet they'd live a lot differently.

—Bill Watterson, *Calvin and Hobbes*

Taking in the vastness of the universe and the beauty
of the stars can bring perspective. If tonight is a clear
night, plan to spend some time outside simply skygazing.
Sketch the moon or the constellations you see.

How do you feel?

As soon as we
wish to be
happier,
we are no longer
happy.

—Walter Landor

Everyone wants to be happy. Believing that whatever we're after will make us happy is what makes us want it. But believing that something outside of ourselves will make us happy begins with the assumption that we're currently not happy and that this can only be cured by things outside of our control. This is a recipe for unhappiness.

Happiness is a choice,
regardless of circumstances.

When you're not feeling particularly happy, think of a joyful moment in your life. Reflect on the details of the moment, feeling the emotions you experienced at the time. How do you feel now? Do you feel happier? Did anything outside of you change?

_____

_____

_____

_____

_____

_____

_____

_____

_____

_____

The next time you wish you were happier,
make the choice to be so.

Comparison is
the thief of joy.

—Theodore Roosevelt

We do it all the time. We look at others' lives and think how easy they have it. Or we focus on how much better our lives could be in the future if only…. But those mindsets rob us of the joy we could experience in the present.

What talents are uniquely yours right now
that can bring you (and others) joy?

Between stimulus and response there is a space. In that space is our power to choose our response. In our response lies our growth and our freedom.

—Viktor E. Frankl

Everyone has habitual responses to certain stimuli. When your partner, friend, boss, or parent presses one of your buttons, you instinctively respond in the same way you always have. In doing so, you perpetuate the situation from which you wish to escape.

With practice, you can change this cycle. In the instant before you respond the same old way, catch yourself, pause for a second, and choose a different response. Your different response can be as simple as doing nothing.

Experiment with a variety of responses as the situations arise to find a response that leads to a more beneficial outcome for everyone involved.

Situation	Response	Outcome

It's only when we truly know
and understand that we have
a limited time on earth—
*and that we have no way of
knowing when our time is up*—
that we will begin to live each day
to the fullest, as if it was
the only one we had.

—Elisabeth Kübler-Ross

According to *The Top Five Regrets of the Dying,* by Bronnie Ware, one of the top regrets is wishing they had the courage to live a life true to themselves, not the life others expected of them. What small change can you make in your daily schedule that allows you to live your life to the fullest, true to yourself and not what others expect of you? Small, daily changes can have a powerful impact.

If it falls to your lot to be a
street sweeper, go out and sweep streets
like Michelangelo painted pictures.

—Martin Luther King, Jr.

What do you love about your career? Make a list.
Think hard and get creative.

_____   _____

_____   _____

_____   _____

What do you dislike about your career?

_____   _____

_____   _____

_____   _____

For each dislike, is it something you can change? How can you
change it? When will you make the change? If you can't change it,
can you see it differently or simply accept it? Without accepting
things and people that you can't change, you're sentencing yourself
to more unhappiness and suffering.

_____

_____

_____

_____

_____

_____

_____

_____

_____

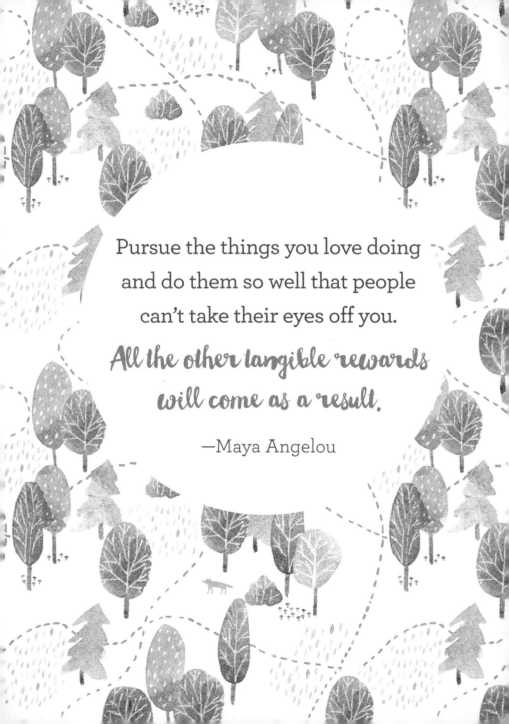

Pursue the things you love doing and do them so well that people can't take their eyes off you. All the other tangible rewards will come as a result.

—Maya Angelou

Can you see yourself doing what you're doing for the rest of your life? If so, how can you do it in a way that makes you even happier? If not, what career/passion/lifestyle could you choose that would lead to a positive answer? Make a list of possibilities.

_____

_____

_____

_____

_____

If all signs lead toward a new path, take the first step now:

- ☐ Contact someone you know who is already doing what you're interested in.

- ☐ Use online research to find someone on a similar path and learn more about that person.

- ☐ Find forums on your passion/career and get involved.

- ☐ Read books on the subject.

Just take a step, *any* step. Acknowledging your passions and giving them the breath of life will lead you to places you never could have planned or expected. And you'll be happier when you give yourself permission to explore.

If you want others
to be happy,
practice compassion.

If you want
to be happy,
practice compassion.

—The 14th Dalai Lama

Compassion allows you to put yourself in the other's shoes, see the world through their eyes, interpret the world through their past experiences. With compassion, you begin to better understand the other person and judge them less harshly.

When you practice compassion with yourself, you can soften all the harsh judgments you've held over yourself, forgive yourself for being imperfect, and love yourself for being who you are without needing to change anything.

What "changes" in others and yourself are you still holding out for that you can let go?

Happiness is letting go of what you think your life is supposed to look like and celebrating it for everything that it is. —Mandy Hale

What dream or vision from the past can you give up,
knowing where you are and what brings you joy today?

_____

_____

_____

_____

_____

_____

_____

_____

_____

_____

_____

_____

_____

_____

_____

_____

_____

_____

The present moment is filled with joy and happiness. If you are attentive, you will see it.

—Thich Nhat Hanh

So often we feel that daily life is the drudgery and that "someday" things will change and life will be much better, more exciting. But daily life is all we have. Our lives are a long string of moments, some more memorable than others.

Mindfulness helps us to see the excitement in the ordinary, the awe in the everyday. By slowing down and noticing the beauty and wonder in what's always around us, every day, we can experience enlightenment.

Head into your day planning a few pauses to consider the simple moments that have touched your soul, or look back on your day before bed.

Morning Moments of Joy

_____

_____

_____

Afternoon Moments of Joy

_____

_____

_____

Evening Moments of Joy

_____

_____

_____

Joy is what happens to us when we allow ourselves to recognize how good things really are.

—Marianne Williamson

Try a different approach today: What concerns or challenges do you *not* have to worry about? For some, finances may not be a concern. For others, there's no worry over family feuds. What areas or situations in your life are safe and good for you?

_____

_____

_____

_____

_____

_____

_____

_____

_____

_____

_____

_____

_____

_____

_____

_____

_____

_____

_____

If you want to conquer
the anxiety of life, live in the
moment, live in the breath.

—Amit Ray

Anxiety is the mind anticipating a negative future. It's a mental "What if?" that's never answered rationally. It's the mind assuming that the only result could be the worst case.

The next time you're feeling anxious, ask yourself how likely the presumed future is. If you feel that the worst case is likely, instead of letting your anxiety swirl around that picture, play out the worst-case scenario.

Ask yourself what would happen if the worst case played itself out. Mentally take the next step, and the next, until nothing else could happen and you realize that you'll be okay.

In the end, just three things matter:

How well we have lived
How well we have loved
How well we have learned to let go.

—Jack Kornfield

Possessions and achievements can dominate our goals.
How important are these things to your core happiness?
How do they contribute to how well you live, love, and let go?

List three ways you have lived well:

1. _____

2. _____

3. _____

List three ways you have loved well:

1. _____

2. _____

3. _____

List three ways you have learned to let go:

1. _____

2. _____

3. _____

Whenever you feel doubts about yourself creeping in,
remember *these* accomplishments.

Sanity and happiness are an impossible combination.

—Mark Twain

Not everything that makes you feel joy needs to serve any other practical purpose. Make a list of activities or things that make you feel happy that might seem a little crazy to someone else. Return to the list for inspiration when you need it!

1. _____

2. _____

3. _____

4. _____   5. _____

6. _____

Do not ruin today
with mourning tomorrow.

—Catherynne M. Valente

How often do you feel anxious or fret about what hasn't occurred yet? How often do you not see the beauty and joy in the present moment because you're worried about the future? Notice the next time you're "mourning tomorrow." In that moment, stop what you're doing, close your eyes, take three deep breaths, and, on a long out-breath, say to yourself, **"Be here now."** Then open your eyes and notice that all is well and beautiful in this moment.

Write the words **"Be here now"** in the space below to own the phrase.

Our challenge each day is not

to get dressed to face the world

but *to unglove ourselves* so that

the doorknob feels cold

and the car handle feels wet and

the kiss goodbye feels like the

lips of another being,

soft and unrepeatable.

—Mark Nepo

Describe some moments of your day in this way—full of rich, feeling adjectives and actions.

Life is a dance.
Mindfulness
is witnessing
that dance.

—Amit Ray

Mindfulness allows you to be what is known as the Observer. The Observer steps outside of yourself and objectively observes your thoughts, your actions, your beliefs. It doesn't judge or criticize. It acts like a curious child.

As you dance through life, you can use your Observer to notice things that previously escaped your attention. These things might be your habitual actions, routines, responses, ways of thinking. Or they might be the people you see each day but hardly notice.

By seeing the world through the eyes of your Observer, you're free to interpret your world differently. In each moment, you're free to make new choices, see what you previously missed, and experience the joy that's always around you.

What totally new sight did you see today or will you see tomorrow?

Perfection of character is this:
to live each day as if
it were your last,
without frenzy,
without apathy,
without pretense.

—Marcus Aurelius

If you knew that today would be your last, how would you spend it? Knowing that you couldn't possibly complete your bucket list or finish everything on your to-do list, what would become your most important things in the last day of your life?

_____

_____

_____

_____

_____

_____

Are you currently living as if these things are your most important? If so, how are you living that? If not, are you willing to make changes that would help you align your days with your most important things?

_____

_____

_____

_____

_____

_____

Few of us ever live in the present. We are forever anticipating what is to come or remembering what has gone.

—Louis L'Amour

The essence of mindfulness is being in the present moment. That means not thinking about the past or the future, only focusing on what is happening right here, right now.

Quickly and without overthinking, jot down a list of twenty things you're noticing in this moment that you're currently experiencing. These can be things like how you're feeling physically or emotionally, specific aspects of the weather or your environment, qualities of the people around you, how you're responding to any of this.

1. _____
2. _____
3. _____
4. _____
5. _____
6. _____
7. _____
8. _____
9. _____
10. _____
11. _____
12. _____
13. _____
14. _____
15. _____

 How many of these can you be grateful for?
Draw a heart next to them.

Don't believe everything you think. Thoughts are just that—thoughts.

—Allan Lokos

Thoughts come and go like clouds passing across the sky. Just like clouds, thoughts pop up suddenly, constantly change and evolve, and eventually dissipate. They may be accompanied by rain, storms, rainbows, and beautiful forms. If you try to capture them, there's nothing but mist.

Given this nature, how can you hold onto thoughts? How can thoughts create walls in which you live? Thoughts can only hold the power over you that you give them. But you can change them in an instant.

Stop a few times throughout your day to notice your thoughts. How much are you allowing them to sway your emotions and actions? Are they bringing you joy? If not, it's up to you to change them, in that moment.

Sketch or describe your thoughts about some of the clouds in your life.

In this moment,
there is plenty of time.
In this moment, you are
precisely as you should be.
In this moment,
there is infinite possibility.

—Victoria Moran

Your conscious mind is probably thinking that this quote is absurd. Plenty of time? There's never enough time. As you should be? There's so much to improve. Infinite possibility? There are plenty of limitations.

Those are thoughts. Thoughts are only true if you believe them to be. You can create any story you like about these factors.

The concept of "not enough time" is based on a projection of the future where everything isn't complete. In this moment, there's plenty of time for what is happening in the moment.

In this moment, if you "should" be anything other than who and what you are, it would be so. The opinions of others as to what you should or shouldn't be are irrelevant.

In every moment there's infinite possibility. Any limitations are those you've chosen to believe.

In this moment, you are perfect as you are, and you have plenty of time to create what you desire. Given this, what choice will you make next?

_____

_____

_____

_____

_____

Respond; don't react.
Listen; don't talk.
Think; don't assume.

—Raji Lukkoor

We all want to be heard, and we usually want to be right. When we react, talk, and assume, we're putting ourselves first without acknowledging the other person. We aren't allowing them to be heard. If you were the other person, how would that make you feel? Given those feelings, how open would you be in the interaction?

Responding, listening, and thinking all require that you pause and consider the other person before choosing a response. All of these choices allow the other person to be heard. If they feel heard, is there a better likelihood that they will pause to listen to you—and that the joy in your relationship will increase?

In your next conversation, notice how often you're thinking of your response while the other person is still talking. Notice the assumptions you're instinctively drawing as they speak. Notice when you're reacting in the same old ways instead of pausing to consider a different way of responding.

All worldly joys are less than that one joy of doing kindnesses.

—John Wesley

We all have gifts to offer to the world. It's your task to figure out what your gifts are and give them. Often your gifts seem too simple. They're simply what makes you uniquely you.

Ask someone close to you who sees you in a positive light what they think your gifts are, the ways that you've helped them or others. How can you offer those gifts on a regular basis?

_____

_____

_____

_____

_____

_____

_____

_____

_____

_____

_____

_____

_____

Restore your attention
or bring it to a new level by
dramatically slowing down
whatever you're doing.

—Sharon Salzberg

Hurrying and multitasking often lead to tasks taking longer than if you had approached them in a relaxed manner.

The next time you're running late, working against a deadline, or feeling rushed, close your eyes and take three deep breaths to calm your mind. Notice the tension in your body and allow it to melt. Then focus on the most important or immediate task at hand until it's complete, doing it well (not perfectly) and in a relaxed manner. Don't think about the other tasks you have to get done or the larger deadline.

How did you feel when you completed the task at hand in a different way? Did it take any longer?

_____

_____

_____

_____

_____

Take a few deep breaths and approach
your next task in the same manner.

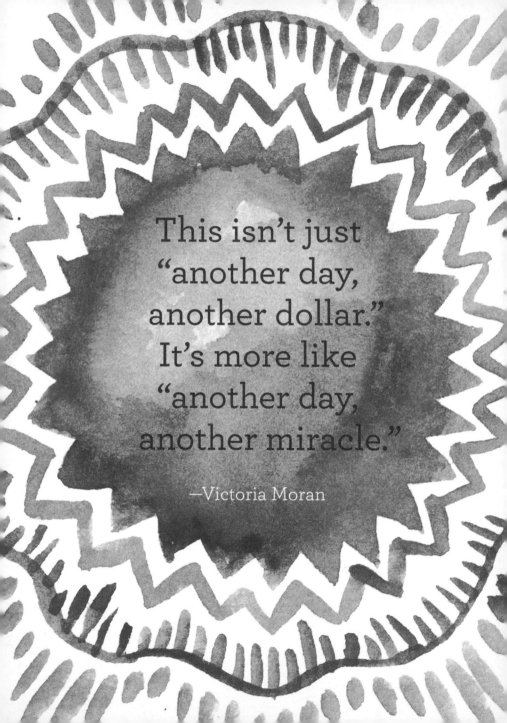

This isn't just "another day, another dollar." It's more like "another day, another miracle."

—Victoria Moran

Every day you're surrounded by miracles large and small. How many do you notice?

The blooming of a flower, the beating of your heart, an amazing sunrise and sunset...everything that must come together to create these experiences makes them everyday miracles. List ten miracles you've experienced lately.

1. _____

2. _____

3. _____

4. _____

5. _____

6. _____

7. _____

8. _____

9. _____

10. _____

collect
moments,
not things.

How do you feel when you spend money? Consider your feelings when you spend money on:

- food
- housing (mortgage or rent)
- clothing
- gifts
- art
- furnishings
- your career or business
- vehicles
- entertainment

- debt
- travel
- charity
- education
- pets
- savings
- medical expenses
- taxes
- fun

Each category probably stirs up different feelings. Notice them.

Think about an upcoming purchase. Notice your feelings about this purchase. Consider such questions as:

- How do I feel right now?
- Am I buying this to placate my feelings, or am I fulfilling a real need?
- How will I feel about this purchase tomorrow, next week, next year?
- Does making this purchase take me away from fulfilling other goals?
- Can I wait to make this purchase?

The perfect time is now.

Finish this sentence: It's been too long since...
(Some examples: I colored with crayons. I played a board game.
I sang in the shower. I bought myself flowers.)

Make a list—and a plan to indulge.

We need never be bound by
the limitations of our previous
or current thinking,
nor are we ever locked into
being the person we used to be,
or think we are.

—Allan Lokos

There's no rule that says you must be the same person you've been in the past. In each moment, you have the opportunity to start making new choices. If you stop thinking that your future is limited by what you've done or who you were, you can fully embrace the opportunities that are always in front of you in the present moment.

What's your vision of an amazing everyday life? Reflect on the kind of person who already lives that life.

Throughout your day, keep that vision in mind and catch yourself when you think like your old self, the self that would say that your perfect day is impossible. Simply notice the thought—don't judge it—and change it to something that supports your vision. The more often you do that and take baby steps toward your perfect day, the faster your dream life will become a reality.

What you focus on expands.

The thoughts you have throughout your day control your emotions and actions. If you think negative things, you'll have negative emotions and find reasons not to take the actions that can change your day (or your life).

You're not a victim of your thoughts. Your emotions don't control you. You have the strength and ability to change them with mindfulness—by simply noticing them when they arise and changing the ones you don't like.

Write down five thoughts that you have about yourself or your world that are not supporting you. Next to each thought, write a new, supportive thought that you will focus on whenever you notice one of the old thoughts arising. Keep this list in plain view in a few places so you can remind yourself of the new positive you're working toward.

Current Thoughts ↓

New Thoughts ↓

1. _____ _____

_____ _____

2. _____ _____

_____ _____

3. _____ _____

_____ _____

4. _____ _____

_____ _____

5. _____ _____

_____ _____

I have found my greatest
moments of joy and peace
just sitting in silence,
and then I take that joy & peace
with me out into the world.

—Holly Mosier

You're a human being, not a human doing. While simply taking time to be can seem like you're not being productive or you're goofing off, the truth is the opposite. By constantly doing, you're wearing yourself thin and only experiencing life on the surface, never diving deep where the joy resides.

Taking time to be isn't selfish. It's another way to care for yourself so that you can be that much better for everyone you serve.

Write down five ways you can make time in your schedule to simply be. Here are some ideas:

»» Walk or sit in nature, noticing the sights, smells, and experience.

»» Soak in a hot bath.

»» Sit with your partner, simply holding hands and noticing your love for the other person.

1. _____

2. _____

3. _____

4. _____

5. _____

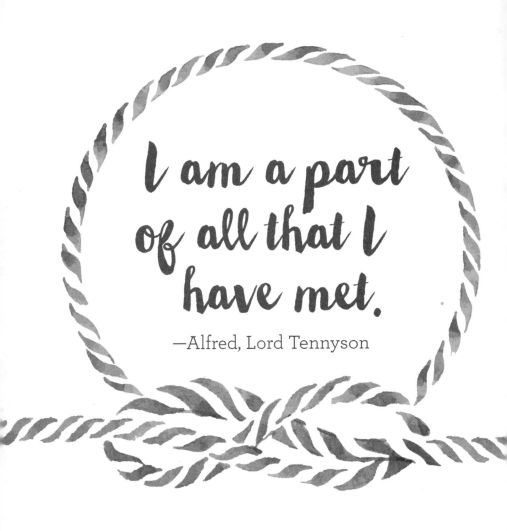

I am a part of all that I have met.

—Alfred, Lord Tennyson

Stop reading and look up. What do you see?
Really look and notice.

If you see other people, look at each person individually. Think about how they might be feeling right now. What is their average day like? What is their life like? How could you help them be a little happier right now? **Do it.**

If you see nature, focus on specifics. What is the temperature like? Is it sunny or cloudy, and how does that make you feel? What do you hear? Notice the trees and plants. How old do you think they are? What have they seen? How can you make your surroundings a little nicer? **Do it.**

If you see animals, wonder about how they experience the world. How can you make them happier? **Do it.**

By interacting with your surroundings instead of making them separate from you, you can better understand how interconnected everything is. This feeling brings joy.

What if we stopped celebrating being busy as a measurement of importance?

What if instead we celebrated how much time we had spent listening, pondering, meditating, and enjoying time with the most important people in our lives?

—Greg McKeown

How much time have you spent in contact with the most important people in your life this week? Tally the hours here.

_____

_____

_____

_____

_____

_____

Not satisfied with the time? What can you do to make more space for your loved ones in the coming weeks?

_____

_____

_____

_____

_____

_____

This
is my
happy
place.

Is there a place that brings you peace?
Draw it or describe it here.

_____

_____

_____

_____

Even when you can't be there physically, go there in your mind to remind yourself what peace feels like. Then hold onto that feeling for the rest of the day.

It's good to
have an end
in mind but in
the end what counts
is how you travel.

—Orna Ross

Choosing to be happy is the journey, not the destination. There is no "someday." There is only today, right now. "Happy" is how we do life, our way of being as we experience our days.

Happiness is the choice to accept life as it comes and make the most of it. Resistance and expectation create unhappiness. Acceptance of everything in life creates happiness. Acceptance of things as they are is the first step toward changing them.

What aspects of your life are you currently resisting? How can you change that resistance to acceptance?

_____

_____

_____

_____

_____

_____

_____

We were together. I forget the rest.

—Walt Whitman

It can help to have someone to reach out to when you're having trouble finding joy.

Whom can you ask to be your partner in your joy journey?

_____

_____

_____

_____

_____

_____

_____

_____

_____

_____

_____

Sometimes you need to talk to a three-year-old so you can understand life again.

Children can offer the perfect example of living in the moment. If you have children in your life, reserve some extra time to chat and play with them. Reflect upon the time you share and what you experience that brings you joy.

_____

_____

_____

_____

_____

_____

How can you fill your daily moments with more kid's-eye views?

_____

_____

_____

_____

_____

_____

_____

Joy does not simply
happen to us.
We have to choose joy &
keep choosing it every day.

—Henri Nouwen